Grace

Michael Davidson

SPUYTEN DUYVIL

New York City

Acknowledgments

Thanks to the editors of journals where some of these poems first appeared: *OBU Manifestos 2, Whiskey and Fox, Action Spectacle, Supplement*. I'd also like to thank Tod Thilleman for his excellent editorial support and to the staff at Spuyten Duyvil for their help in making *Grace*. Finally, a big thanks to Joseph Grigely for his cover image and for his conversations over the years.

Library of Congress Control Number: 2025933129

for Arlo and Shiloh

                                                    Grace
        to be born and live as variously as possible

                            (Frank O'Hara)

Contents

GRACE

Voice

Post Script   105

Grace is a manner, an aesthetic of tact, but to navigate an ableist world also requires tactics. Michael Davidson has perfected a postmodern lyric whose deft shifts in tone and syntax parse a changing present in which climate crisis and social media coincide with aging and gradual deafness. His poems register how it feels to enter "the social/as a stave of differences." And though they document the "catalogue of affect" that arises from embodied difference, they also aim to meet error and misunderstanding with generosity and crip wit. Reading *Grace*, I'm reminded that "language has no solitude" when a poet is this good.

Brian Teare, author of *Poem Bitten By a Man*

Michael Davidson's acclaimed work in disability studies takes a deeply personal turn in *Grace*, whose sharply chiseled lines and stanzas "chronicle a period of gradual hearing loss that began in the mid 1990s and continues into the present day." "[W]hat is left when sound dies" leads to what he calls "a poetics of error"—"big not pig, / cat not hat," "'A' becomes 'F'," the articulation of sound in words disappearing into a "drone [that] captures silence in its slithery net." Swimming in the ocean, which for years has been a regular part of Davidson's life on the coast of Southern California, becomes "paddling down to the littoral . . . tuning on that low drone [that] locks the body into itself." That body becomes "a hollow" in which "words flower (follow) as if you are having a conversation with yourself." Other "matter[s] of attention" appear in other poems—"the baby bombed in the hospital"; "March / . . . full of loss, first L

/ then T now M / their thisness / pressed between leaves / a variable life"; the "algorithm / [that] tells you what you need"; the "miracles" one sometimes gets to see in nature ("owl guarding its nest / next to the lagoon / whimbrel pecking in sand"). All of this and so much more made present in the "hard surface" of Davidson's language, which variously "embraces all the flaws," makes *Grace* must reading for everyone who cares about our precarious condition in the world as well the "news," as Williams called poetry, "that stays news."

Stephen Ratcliffe, author of *m o m e n t*

"Between the motion/And the act/Falls the shadow," wrote T.S. Eliot long ago. In *Grace* Michael Davidson explores this shadowy intervening space with less drama and, in my opinion, more grace than Eliot did, looking for what connects and disconnects us. When we converse, for instance, we don't simply exchange words. It's also the case that:

............silences
must be inspected for what must not
be mentioned, but considered
for the conversation to continue.

Clearly this is a tricky, delicate business. Davidson, who has experienced and adapted to severe hearing loss, knows quite a lot about inhabiting the gaps between speech and understanding, or, as he puts it, "…the hiatus before the image." Like Creeley, he has heard "words full of holes." It is the job of the poet to attend to such spaces and Davidson does this masterfully. *Grace* speaks to this moment when, it seems, we are all losing the ability to hear one another. It may be my personal favorite among Michael Davidson's numerous books.

Rae Armentrout

Few poets incite in me such measured quiet as Michael Davidson, who lends in this collection his signature voice to agile rumination: what does it mean to reposition oneself in regard to the materiality of language as access to that material shifts? Through descriptive engagement and lyrical association—which may vibrate differently in readers who are deaf or hard-of-hearing—Davidson recounts with patience the fickle nature of sonics and the intimacies therein. These poems balance insight and erasure from within the intellectual and emotional generosity of vulnerability; Davidson has created in *Grace* a stunning blend of both attention to and desertion of sound, weighing equally what is lost and what is gained.

Meg Day, author of *Last Psalm at Sea Level*

Michael Davidson fulfills the promise of 'a new knowledge of reality': a ghostly "audiogram" of deafness, deftly conjuring poems of incarnate difference. His "fall into language" is both a failing and flailing into grace. It is raised: a social body.

Charles Bernstein

Presence

"I did not wish to be brought to life, and I am greatly ashamed of my conglomerate personality"

(The Gump in *The Marvelous Land of Oz*)

THE PLAUSIBLE SUBJECT

An owl at 3:00 a.m.
saying who,
it could have been me,

sleep replaced
with "unrebuked consciousness"
(let's run through the pronouns),

cars on the freeway
a kind of sighing subject,
hearing them

is a ground
as an ear becomes
what I must be

when asleep,
feeling nothing yet
carrying on the unending

conversations, who
to whom.

CENOTAPH

A death in the family takes the form of this form,
what follows is outside the frame
since events refuse the categories
they are given
and chatter back from the grave at the indecency
of their memorial like the small notebook
in which one records the dream
that never quite coincides
with anyone yet bears a striking resemblance
to D or M who appear in cameo roles
along with the spaces since we last met—
a dark bar in Vancouver, the park in Perugia,
memories of misspent youth
etched on this cenotaph
one dreams is my own;
I, too, lived in Leucadia
among the palms and condos,
midway on this highway
I was interrupted by the body
that consumes everything,
it was a dark wood I was
a small death waiting to be born.

APOPHASIS IN PUBLIC

In the interests of fair play
I won't say anything too critical
of the null who occupies our speech,

this is one way of avoiding the fact
that we hide in signs of assurance
the germ of our extinction,

and we fail,
but failure is a kind of renewal, even
(and this is the exciting part)

another occasion to talk
despite the crash of other voices
and music in the background,

what he means by that
cannot be verified
by any appeal to its subject,

a cadaver is also meat,
blue is a shaded green,
China can be reinvented

as the latest version of ourselves
where "our" means not me,
cigarettes were lit, lights dimmed

when we were social, now
there are no more cigarettes, rooms
or conversations, "if"

is a tunnel into "would,"
if he appears at the scene after the fact
would he have caused it

or would have
wearing such dubious clothing
and distinctive hair?

the less of us on the street
the more he occupies space
and the words in between.

BUNDLED AFFECT

She has thrown the fork,
I am left to think about it for a day,
entire sentences go unprovoked, they stop
and then start up again

like a dog scratching its fleas,
the impact of a thrown word
makes the others unnecessary:
door, gun, flesh, ear, pill, person,

feeling is not alone
but a void in which we walk
without headlights, that poppy
has no intention,

a person on the other hand
(and then Stalin walks out
during the love scene),
we are left to explain intention

as the result of something forgotten,
the news is not good,
a man in Texas has a new penis,
the courts refuse to agree

on conception, his misdeeds
follow him through the next decades
which he incorporates
into his memoirs, no one

is at fault yet the feeling persists, folding
itself around incident long gone,
it penetrates the filament thin membrane
we once called consciousness

(trigger warning
some of these images may inspire
longing) I, too, left the room
unable to complete the sentence,

too old to manage toggles
that move these repetitions towards a body,
Jack hides under the table
while the giant counts his gold,

in all these stories we are moved
by forces beyond our control
a beanstalk appears in the garden,
it carries us into the upper world,

and the sign says don't
take it personally, I write this
but can't hear my voice,
it sounds like a waterfall.

THE PRESENT 1

I remember the event
because of a photo
that explains how I came
to be there in the transition

between living
and dining room as my father,
so it was explained,
returned from the war

as vividly as if it happened
that way and thus merged
into anecdotes I use
in place of the present

that escapes me, there was
the marble top highboy,
a framed set of teacups
hats on a high shelf

in boxes because
women wore hats,
what is certain is this recurring
sentence that begins

I remember the event

THE PRESENT 2

We're worn out by the normal,
trying to live up
to what escapes us
but that everyone else

discusses with ease,
they hear each other
exchanging ideas
about that ottoman,

and at the pharmacy
the machine
refuses to accept a bar code
and requires someone

to intervene, this bar of soap
is not necessary to the social,
but in its exchange
something like the present

becomes present,
you recognize its passing
as you head to the exit,
the odor of verbena follows

you out the door.

THE PRESENT 3

Vacant practices
like tying shoes in the forest
or soul clapping hands
to ward off thinking about it,

you have already felt the needle
before its life-affirming prick,
a life-affirming tale
of better things to come,

the dream has condensed this scene
long before arriving
at whatever diagnosis
has made living bearable,

you find yourself
in a room trying to remember
what you hoped to find there,
you have mastered the sign for hope

but forgotten the one for spleen,
a moment of indecision
followed by a moment
of indecision,

hand me that hammer.

The Present 4

It's true what they say,
we'd like to arrive at last
at the present,
gather oneself in its folds

like a warm blanket
in the operating room, then
we could at last experience
not fearing pain, not

wanting better acoustics,
that light the lamp cast
in the light store,
but

what becomes of the dream?
you're late for the train,
the one in which one is not
Jeremy Prynne,

or last night, the endless search
for a restaurant in a warren
of streets, what tense
is without time, a sign

etched on the body
they say must be preserved
against desire
and the objects that explain it

almost successfully?

THE PRESENT 5

The heat is becoming normal,
we search for shade
as part of eating food,
the part in which ingestion

coincides with sleep
and other events of forgetting;
in neighborhoods where shade
is not an option

no one exists
no one sits in sun at the bus stop
with a small child fussing,
not existing is becoming normal

and can be reenacted
in a new genre, call it
relevant distractions:
you put on that blue shirt

eat those yellow eggs
watch that screen
the one in which your friends
disappear as you scroll down,

fire burns in other places
where we do not live,
that is their story, the pronoun
that keeps us on course, the one

that finds shade.

MOCKINGBIRD

Break open the common phrase,
for to be awake
is to see it otherwise; I saw a desert at dawn
from a hurtling Mercedes, I heard a ping
when the screen went black, heard words
full of holes; knocking at the door,
a white shirt selling the goods,
then we had memory
which we attacked with distraction,
music was articulate space
with lyrics of endless life, the road
and the rice, the press and the pen, distance
was not impossible, I'll get back to you
when the sun is up; one mockingbird
is protecting the world from itself
repeating the word for myself.

I'M HAVING ONE OF THOSE SOL LEWITT DAYS

nothing on the inside, nothing outside,
fuchsias drip over the redwood box,
numbers fit into place as things
and things are more than their corners,
that reference to the hammer
has been useful but impractical,
send me the bill;

Poussin pink hovers over Marine Corps base,
small puffs of smoke rising from the fake
Arab village, this transcription
will begin in a moment;

errors should not be attached to a person;

sky and sea converge at the horizon
where the idea of speech begins,
I love speech,
so many boxes to fill.

PENCIL

Remember the pencil?
a yellow inducement,

and the blank page,
remember that?

now filled with letters
and spaces of little interest,

the more they arrive
and fill in the blanks

with their endless palaver
the more a sky resigns

to be its mirror, the page
remains alive, alert, says

try again to erase
that dream, that offense

of youth, try
again the stylus

by which we forget
to grow old, remember?

The Black Sun

In this dream I kill two friends,
stuff them into a cereal box,
covering the top with plastic wrap
and wait until the shaking stops,

later, I hug another friend goodbye
though she is going nowhere,
the sky is full of smoke,
the lake a sheet of mercury;

it's the forest's fault
that trees grow close together
to exchange notes
and express affection,

they must be exterminated,
the dream writes this
almost without effort
as the settlement rises

out of vacant land,
and in Vegas
quarters are fed into a machine,
but it's the wrong machine,

the attendant says that's the slot
for bills not coins, trees
speak a slow language
no one understands,

fire begins here
in a sentence no one is permitted
to complete, the next dream
is the black sun.

STIPULATIONS

you must think we are absolute

    (idiots, dolts, naïfs, patsies, enablers, Pollyanna's

for the way we have handled

    (our youth, your youth, their future, his likelihood of

and appeared to endorse

    (trickle down, normative gender, racial stereotypes

under the umbrella of

    (tolerance, self-interest, empathy, financial accountability

while supporting

    (redistribution, free speech, slow food, indigenous rights

that are being coopted by

    (social media, free speech, neoliberal repayment

under the guise of

    (fairness, accommodation, consensus, rational choice

because

    (you require us, we feed you, reality sucks, people have lost touch

and in another life

    (we wouldn't be having this, we will forget, you'd move back home,
    we'd be dead

where

    (we had a choice, fate hadn't delivered a bad hand, you suddenly
    "got it"

we could go on

    (living, perpetuating this oppressive relationship, eating rich food

and not think any further about

    (qualifications, unanticipated events, monsoons, suicide bombers,
    the gun lobby

that your

    (outrage, repressed feelings, lies, subterfuges, late night tweets have reinforced in our

      (insecurity, muted anger, resignation, suicidal thoughts
that we depend on if

      (our youth, your youth, their future, his likelihood of
we're to

      (live together, emigrate, share our resources, keep on talking

Rooms (after James Castle)

Using a pointed stick, soot
and spit
he drew interiors
of sheds, out buildings, coops

shelves and rafters forming
the grid and through doors or windows
looked back and out
into Idaho, he never spoke

nor apparently heard but in shades
of grey made structure
speak back, he liked to work
the milk separator.

DISTRESSING AIR

We're living in the monsoon
where the air is wet and the sea seasonally
warm out near the yellow buoy,

a dog is whining next to the anthologies
where silence is lodged
between the lines,

I don't mean that blank
that follows a siren
but what replaces ellipses,

is it midge or fruit fly?
a mote floats around the fruit bowl
the eye's concave mirror,

her cat of 21 years
takes her breath away
as they dies,

it is difficult becoming
a plural,
bitcoin achieves a new record

for the sake of the future's
trumpeting heroics,
the beds are filled

with breathing, freedom
is bitcoin: believe in it
or die,

I digress
but I have not begun.

THE PIOUS DAUGHTER-IN-LAW'S SOUP
(AFTER REN PENG NIAN)

He begins to smoke
to lighten his depression,
isolated
he is stoned by local children,
slowly
he climbs a flight of stairs;

when a photo is taken of him
he looks back reproachfully
as though excluded;

the revolution has not dismissed me
the people have not dismissed me
and I have not dismissed myself;

she says ironically
why not go to the US,
you can sit in a big car
and do naked dances.

Sustainable Growth

Money then pollen then soprano,
I come to this valley as an oracle of lunch,
show me the rooster, the corn that lives after death
show me the flesh dissolving into laughter
(carbon becomes broccoli), the "eureka moment"
with its fiery altar and federal thing
because after all and without which
arable land burns and
burning is another word for replace,
like the place we burned the tar-soaked word,
smoke and the revised eclogue
called mortgage, I used to sit on this rock
and the sea shattered into tinsel,
I used to be the afflatus, morpheme into fire,
one thing becomes one thing
and someone gets paid, O
"whither shall we fly?"

Drone

"Grammar is on your face"

(Christine Sun Kim)

My Audiogram

Must sing in the night
fragrant decibels, jasmine, lilac,
a river of pitches rustles
below the bridge, Kyrie

begins in the basses and rises
into the invisible Credo,
notes are the text
of distant listening,

what they say
is beyond me: big not pig
cat not hat,

the body enters the social
in a stave of differences.

GHOSTS

"He's none of *me*, even as I *might* have been"

(Henry James, "The Jolly Corner")

Ghosts don't talk so good
they mumble and gibber
especially in restaurants
where the acoustics are terrible,

they once lived
in bodies of language, words
etched on tongues
we could read;

everyone cranes their necks
to see them at the next table,
but they're on the other side
of seeing,

we want confirmation
of what they want,
possessed as they say
by a word that escapes us.

RETURNING SILENCE
(AFTER VELASQUEZ)

It's quiet where the world ends
and the head begins,
a soft padding across carpets
and the room disappears,

distance dissolves into light and light
falls equally upon the painter
and the dwarf when the world stops
and the head turns in upon itself,

because what is left
is the mirror, figures dimly seen
on the back wall, and shards of voice
banging against the tympanum

that becomes the studio, a stream
of conversation
roaring against bare walls,
what is left when sound dies

is time in a mirror
of these words turning their backs
on the world, the court,
and the dwarf at the margin

who measures the center.

ECHOLALIA

An unused phoneme drifts into memory
after the barbarians have come from the north
or precedes the name of God
in one of the forbidden books,

we scream
at the checkout stand, it stops
a crying child, a child crying
utters the name of God

by the watermelons,
I used to love the body
that now speaks through hands
of uncertain gravity:

retrieve, restore, the sign for
back and the pinched Adam's
apple of curiosity
and the absent corpus

its multiple orifice
a vessel of succor, no sound
(wound) could not be spoken,
no pain unaccounted,

at night,
one shouts at the memory
of lost flesh, lost songs
the lure of their retrieval

like the distant H
a ghost of breath
once wholly body now
a distant glacier

melting into air.

DESTROYED PITCH

Between a rock and a second rock
ticking on a reef,
A becomes F,
I love difference
that flattens into billiards clacking
on an infinite felt, memory says
the opening bars
ascend in thirds
but how to know when pitch drowns
into throbbing water, one is under sound,
that little downward figure
or the trill just after the opening
when the dotted notes return
to the main theme, no wonder "Prussian,"
(the king was a good cellist)
cantabile in the lower register,
that rumbles in the inner ear,
shock absorbers or poor alignment
on a rough road,
where is pitch when it dies in a field
of undifferentiated timbre? these clinks
and rumbles come back in silence
with sound, I just heard
the little waltz in the 2nd movement
for a passing moment.

DRONE

A robust and boisterous clamor for noise
in pitches against this gray drone,
where bleak departs from fleck or belt, inflection
is a distant horizon: I roast peppers
interrogative is not I roast peppers,
yet they stay inflecting air;

in three weeks, this steroid panopticon
stares back at a largely visual display
with the occasional pop of a door or ping
of some timer telling me fish,
a phantom stands oddly poised in the doorway
oddly human;

so that verbs fall away, why use them
to describe motion when objects fall on your head
and make a hollow noise? The drone
captures silence in its slithery net
and disperses water around the cochlea,
the shell hears the sea they say;

but humans are phantoms, holding money
and desire through conversation, their shirts
crinkle with gladness, their skirts rustle
in a novel, the sex scenes used to be on my side
now they lie on the page, hugging the margin
of a once body now mannequin;

waking in fog, padding down
to the machine I dream
of tires rumbling over macadam, cherries
crunched and Janacek, *Intimate Letters*,
so quiet without pitch yet vigorous
in pursuit of dance and nation;

I defer to those clanking guts
that growl in the lower registers,
and claw their way through the exostoses
and then to Idaho, dream of diving
into clear water over millefeuille
to swim in a rhythm of one's stroke;

this is intimacy one speaks through
and reciprocated makes a noise,
the body is a hollow
and words flower (follow) as if you are having
a conversation with yourself,
it is a gray alphabet, but you get to choose.

Access Knowledge

Where to sit,
in a corner preferably
and not next to "him" who mutters
but "her" whose medium pitch

and mobile lips, eyes filling in
the blanks, is speech;
grammar is on your face and face
extends this period

into space,
I remember
when that song
in the *Rückert Lieder*

disappeared into silence,
Teresa von Stade
in a wood lined hall, my life
began in a record store,

it continues silently,
walnut tree shading the grass
and a dog lying beneath
eyeing an orange cat

stealthily avoiding,
and those conversations
that are a distant memory,
a body pauses

on the brink
of a new clause
that may or may not be the conclusion
one had expected, but still

something continues, pollen
falling through hot, clear air,
and the lake's surface
mottled, moving.

DEAF STRUCTURES

We're not so lonely
now that we are home,
one of us has lit the fire, the other
has made up the bed,
I forgot the black bag and had to return
to fetch it, you are the one
I want to hear.

I was introduced as a famous pronoun
and they let me pass,
the cobbled streets were wet
because the movie was wet, I climbed
the stairs to an apartment
in the quarter reserved for darkness,
the hall was dark, the language
difficult to speak,
but others spoke and seemed content
to share their experience,
we can't make out the words,
but their faces tell us we are safe, sorry
querulous,

it's good to know where home is
and the light switch next to the door.

Cockroach

This poem is riddled with verbs,
one hid under the soap dish
another troubles my sleep,
they have survived millennia

of disrespect and volcanic
eruption, the fig
died this summer; we're thinking
of replacing it with...

because life can't be suppressed
by a simple reference to God,
you need to take a walk
see the rocks, big as buildings

(example below), and it all connects
to something I forget which,
the poet wants us to feel
something she has experienced

like Vesuvius or grilled
figs and ham, fog
came in this morning,
buoys at seven second

intervals, this is an example
of odd attentions
modified by rhetoric, I can't
find my key, I can't

hear the timer.

SAY AGAIN 1

I have been reading this book about nothing
until it begins to represent something,
if you wait long enough
goldfish will rise to the surface,

I hear crickets in the bookcase
or an alarm in the ceiling
calling for a new battery,
we are desired by things

and accommodate them
by making sure the rock
is not flesh, not a verb
that we then throw at Him

who must be a rock
that can be killed,
the conversations
are always agreeable,

the man on the phone selling "house"
is also selling "hose" or "hearse,"
I utter the words for smile
and hang up;

the world of articulate voices
is always over there
beyond the rock shaped like a bear
where tourists stop to have their picture

taken so they will not be confused
with a bear or rock,
for now
this is how I see things

but I could be wrong.

Say Again 2

I'm beginning the next phase called
the intermittent, I stop
answering the phone
and take up typing (again)
since what they say is on a screen,
and the screen
is what you know;

adjusting the device I say,
can you fix this vacuum cleaner?
yes, but mauvaise plunk this plastic blunt
not possible bitter next week bring
palabra optimal borkish OK
I say and sign
the form: attention is life;

this must be narrative
I've been here before
the familiar end-stopped line
next to billboard, *They Live*
by Night, we're on the lam
and language follows
fated love;

life inside is quiet
roaring forks and glasses shatter
conversations at the next table
duck confit
on white puree,
a waiter lights a candle,
someone clinks a glass for silence:

padding down to the littoral
I adjust the gogs and shuffle
through shallows, a ray
skitters away while the drone
hovers overhead, one
is watched while diving
under a wave;

to swim from matins
to compline, never missing
a stroke but tuning on that low drone
locks the body into itself
as a tympanum, stroke upon stroke,
I remember pitch
and the voices that surround it.

Only Error

I love Data Week
surgical removal of passwords
one is exhausted but sensual,
documents shredded in a fit of rage
trucks lined up at the border

the solitude of advancing age
yes
what *should* a person be?
salary negotiable
lodging and food included

substituting a word
for a word at the edge

***

our emotions are not ours,
I applied but was rejected
since becoming another person,
we are learning to remain silent
waiting for the room to reveal itself,

the new notebook promised a new
point of view, a dog stopped
in the middle of the street and stared,
fingers and thumb are the same
but their relation to 'M' has changed

a leaf hung from the garage door,
traffic at a standstill.

***

none of us is a material whole
I see you across the room, waving,
the letter 'M' has become painful,
he drops his pen
and begins speaking

his corporeal envelope was well stuffed
with memories, we move among
several persons smiling as appropriate,
the painted birdhouse ignored
by the painted birds

sleep offers an occasion to return
to a terminal, nothing leaves or arrives

***

We're spherical people,
keep signing
while descending,
gophers are eating the fig trees
mounds of loose dirt

the Shell sign at night
harvest moon on wet streets,
trees worry about their health
and send warnings to their neighbors,
a waxing crescent is also a chin

I misunderstand everything,
there's a 'v' at my forehead

***

The body is a cipher
awaiting articulation,
I know you're in there,
they had no words for it
leaving the cave at dawn

a portable desk
out of Styrofoam and cardboard
on which the mystic writing pad
and the letters lost
along with their intentions

what darkness makes plain
light shatters

***

played by the wind
across a casement window
an interstitial music
partly mine
partly its

the Pacific Trash vortex is coming,
troops
take reactor,
what
intellectual breeze

blows across this garden?
the cells listen

***

petulance is not a politics,
the cat piano is not cat art
though their cries are political
hand me those earphones
as we go into the chamber

she wants to own the artist
no one may touch him
I was there first
the ocular harpsichord
that played colors

was never constructed,
build a wall

***

Felix culpa
the errors pile up
until the missing pin is found,
we are made of expectations
others fashion

a lady vanishes
the passengers deny her existence
on their way to somewhere,
he explained falling in the mud
to the passersby who stopped

to help, it's nothing,
gravity is treacherous

***

this patented skin cream
declining into youth,
I am revealed
by my griffonage,
all that's left,

humans go on remembering,
electricity puts an end to this,
literature in 26 letters
they are free to babble
Nietzsche's typewriter

then I became a voice
having written one in a book

***

body of probabilities
two candles on a table
one of us does the wash
one of us has been cancelled
whose name does not appear

he wanted to transform sound
into color, color
into words for ardor
bodies with hands tied
lay in the former street

next to the former school
only error survives

COLOR THEORY

Faces form across the grid, many facets
of erasure and events that follow,
nothing satisfies like an effaced word
where the memory it evokes languishes
in its fragments, the antecedent
has lost its way in a forest of columns,
that's the pleasure in error, we find ourselves
as otherwise and walk in that direction;

she calls it "Interference" and blanks out
certain letters, what had been a word
is replaced by stuff
a word eliminates, bunny
in the backyard eating grass,
dogs herding in Colorado, a brilliant
yellow oriole has returned for a bath,
it's Wednesday it says here;

"help" is inflected for person
or person dissolves into verb,
what's left is a fist on a palm
that moves among present company
needing care, pencils, tea, the idea
of color inspired by a greenish yellow
in a red book, color is idea
taking shape around this slate cup;

in the dream faces appear to speak,
colorless words, misplaced notes
from which he improvises a speech
on a topic he forgets: how to swim
without water, how to sing
without ears, the audience drifts away,
he is left explaining himself to his host
who is also moving away;

hope, on the other hand, is one hand
waving at the other as though we are leaving
on different trains,
the skin is a grid of desire for things
hope is helpless to describe, supreme
in its ardor, desire has no plan
no chance of arriving safely,
"it's worth it to keep one's eyes open,"

color is fingers at the chin
where the fruits and vegetables live,
a garden of face, the nouns
(apple, onion, garlic) form around it
like a halo in Lorenzetti, spirit
is God erased, you have to touch the body
to get a reaction,
see this blue potato?

In Transit

The flesh of words eats into the dreamlife,
missing the last train
and the bathroom door is locked, Istanbul
is a warren of stray cats, the 'f' of foreign
is at the elbow, far
from the sign for forget, I forget
the agreement between speech
and that other thing;

we listen to the screen
announcing the next station,
we watch a face in a movie
without sound, solitude begins
as inconvenience, dissolves into habit,
the Mermaid sells her voice
the Tin Man needs a heart,
we feed on lack like a comparison between

Our Lady of Perpetual, tell me
if someone deserves this skin of stasis
in a station, promising fields of lavender,
a prospect of Eton College while
stuck in traffic, darkness, hunger,
it's like this: lost in transit
with a map of Lodz in winter,
time resembles the Parthenon
a dome of resemblance;

arriving in France, no word
takes me there, but remembering the Gare
one arrives, its portes discharging pilgrims
from Fontainbleu, oysters
across the street and sole meunière,
the revolution not far away
across from the Opera;

what is the sign for social,
an 's' circles an index

language has no solitude

Grace

I've known her—from an ample nation—
Choose One—
Then—close the Valves of her attention—
Like Stone—

(Emily Dickinson)

LEVIATHAN

"The field of mutilation extends indefinitely"
(Henri-Jacques Stiker)

I was standing under this blue image
requested by the reviewer
and saw in the distance a green forest,
I'll stop now

and consider distance as a kind of affection
something that sticks to something else
(affliction, for example); if only
he would provide us with an object

these mutations would seem less arbitrary,
but once you remove a leg or arm
you instantly think of how to put it all back
together in your own image,

and society mumbles approval,
strengthening resolve; you could do pathos
as a backup and have empathy
in time for tea, the body

extended becomes Leviathan,
everything under heaven belongs to me,
I won't fail to speak
of his limbs, his graceful form, etc.

from this remove
we witness the red sun setting
in a comfortable painting
that has never known weather,

and these Euclidian dresses
on the Grande Jatte
enclose their wearers as water
becomes the medium we breathe,

I know it's a stretch
but bodies tend to stop at the edge
of image and blend into each other
in an impasto of skin,

you can't see all of it from here
but move along its flank, piecing together
the flesh you left behind
with the image of flesh before you,

they want you to return the damaged body
to the library of disappointments
so it can disappear in the general catalogue
this image sustains,

a monster rising from the hills,
his body a mosaic of faces
turned away; we only see the giant
face of power over the commons.

The Catalogue of Affect

Having arranged the glasses
by number, having
alphabetized letters
by sender, the senders

by meals shared
in summer, by rivers, or at the edges
of public squares,
having forgotten actors

in the book of actors
or the plots involving a phone
in the night, the scene
of a lost family member

in a familiar guise, having
forgotten the theaters,
art deco pillars and purple lights,
heaven stretched across a ceiling

studded with stars,
I await the feelings that come
and their attachments
to others, objects, rooms

and the expectant audience
that is a body,
an organ of indecision,
meanwhile the worm

still attached to the nerve
nibbles from inside the brain's
dead husk
so that upon waking

I clear my throat to see
if I can hear breathing, click
to hear a message ping,
we are not

this body of skin,
alluvial brain, rhythmic blood
but catalogue of affect for those
ghosts in the margin

as yet unmet, unloved,
all of the conversations yet
to have had and having heard
someone appears at the airport

not having heard her name
that appears in a notebook
I have forgotten to read
have yet to buy

which is partly the blood speaking
through its ample protein,
the voice of what I might have been
had I remembered to write it down

and the other attachments that need
to be filed: the lizard called John
the dog fidgeting in a dream
the cities with bridges

and cities without bridges,
I am unraveling
and those in my wake
are waving toward pyres of light.

Seining

I seine urgencies through this light corridor
blue upon blue to the far buoy and, refreshed,
am open to errancy, talk, lunch;
these cumulous pile at the hills in undulant

and glaucous portals into the sublime (substitute
Visa application) and with password
move forward on the leash of intention
as described in this leaflet from Parmenides,

it's one or the other, the body in pain
flanked by the skeptic in denial
or the body by Mary
Baker Eddy floating like a double

negative through trees and halls
in which I diminish metabolism
to a fine spray, not worth opening
an umbrella yet in this humid

and late season damp what was postponed
now announces its claim, bills
come due, you cancel intentions
and close the flap on Camp Blunt

because an endless period beckons, part
carrot part cart, hard to know
which end of the centaur you sing from,
but the voice, heard in the morning

despite the silences of August
appears to be mine, your response
to this post will confirm the cloud
on which it is written.

Provisional Certainties

I look in the box marked "save"
and find the file "inutile"
for which I appear to have been searching
since the last dream of leaving,

I am perpetually late
and write my address
on an envelope enclosed
in a second envelope, there are no stamps

no pen, we are celibate
in a world at war, intimacy
has been ruled ineffective
or perhaps "inoffensive," the Court

has a ruling somewhere
in a language no one speaks,
I hate to be obtuse
but what is a flail for?

I saved the receipts
for our trip to the desert,
you set up the tent in the wind
while I boiled water,

we shared a language, read Stendhal
in the rain, now
I tie my shoes, wincing
over a body that has learned to live

less itself than idea
and a little dog
trotting at my heels,
it must be

time to roll up the sky
and alphabetize the Gods
according to their ability to sanction grace,
we who were once chosen

must file a request
to speak with the concierge,
there are no more rooms
and the passage vacant

at the Hotel Chopin,
but the city is based on a map,
and each night we enter the labyrinth
untutored in acronyms

that may refer to us,
in the park
portals of memory can be seen
through the mist,

on the opposite side of the lake,
a small boat with a red sail
is on its way
into the present.

Auto Erotic

"When I'm nervous I'm narrative"
(Lyn Hejinian)

Mostly I think of what people do not say
about me when we are talking
about someone else whose silences
must be inspected for what must not

be mentioned but considered
for the conversation to continue,
that incident in the car

or a dumb remark redeemed
only by a lapse of time returns
and prompts this silence into speech
of which I am not its subject

but, in time, in solitude become.

Sometimes I Hear Things

including factories as well as imperatives,
something comes in one door and leaves
by the faint impression of indigence
that blue suits and brown shoes
rise in elevators to prevaricate, look down
and squish in flakey pastry,
but wait! if you've been waiting
for a belt that fits, a mop that flips
then back to the news, it's China
so cute with its smoke and flags,
an entire "we" is being invented
around its emergence as a thing,
I'd like to put it in a nesting doll
but failure is an option, always open;

I'm running to repurpose whatever
these words are, but time
is a receiver that writes down
what has already flown, folks
get a new chip, buy a blender,
each of these products can be obtained
by a process of elimination,
and what
is a potato's relation to society?
the answer is upside down on the final page,
a poet finds its absence in the movement
to an industrialized economy, flush
with junk everyone wants;

I want some consolation
yet factories no longer offer
that faint effluent of sulfur so olfactorily
of a piece with the riparian landscape
that we nearly drove off the road
traveling through midlife and smoke haze,
chicken is wrapped so I know
what it is,
you know what I mean, small pieces
of life lift off from what is left over
and glitter in the ozone.

SHIBBOLETH

I don't do fear,
it's not appetizing
but anxiety,
is always in the next room
sampling the hors d'oeuvres;

if I were without the body
encased in amber
dreams of missing the train
would bruise the flesh
as it passes;

one of your friends
became invisible, the phone
left off the hook back
when there were phones,
when the sound first began
and continues among one of us;

a history of error
could be written with a mirror,
in *der Zwerg* the dwarf sees himself
and dies, holding a white rose,
the courtiers continue to celebrate
their perfect grammar;

falling among rocks
is not an error, failing
to pronounce the correct word
is the condition of exile,
I fall into language, its hard surface
embraces all the flaws;

owl guarding its nest
next to the lagoon
whimbrel pecking in sand
a flotilla of coots near the shore,
how can emptiness
invent these miracles?

On the Verge of Extinction

satisfies the belief that things will get better,
so buy that thing promising sex
in a choice of colors, sizes, death
has never seemed so attractive
now that the earth
can see its shadow, boats marooned on sand,
the sky seen through a skein of wires
and fog, a feeling for leaving
followed by the sensation of traffic,
why bother going out? books
are on the shelf,
beer is in the fridge,
someone displays her hair for an instant
before removing her head in deference,
gestures of salvage melt
along with the glaciers,
at least these provisional certainties
offer a solace once confirmed by grace,
the priests who have an answer
wait until the Sabbath, the election,
the second coming, meanwhile
the Great Auk
is having its last molt
in a book by Audubon
that will live forever.

The Antecedent

Combing through the archive
I came upon oneself,
the wide frames
of glasses one wore
before the wall came down
and those feelings of shame
that we call history, we
who have surmounted desire
live in a cul de sac
surrounded by feelings
that only the font recalls
and even then, foolscap
flakes in yellowed files;

it was the beginning of ends
and the end of ideas
that organized excess
into frames of reference,
of reference into grids,
those pocket parks
that dot the zoning plan
promise relief; the stranger
at the boarding gate
was both friend and agent
of the state, the state
could not weather change
and wrote it
into the plan,
there were files;

one forgets the details
of meals and the conversations
they make possible,
friends dying too soon
of an unknown cause,
friends with a first child
their sleepless nights,
the Utopia he promised
is mired in committee,
let us retire to a safe zone
and vote again,
the Messiah has been delayed
but promises to name
his antecedent;

memory starts at the temple
moves out to a fist,
a sign flies out, returns later
in the philology of dreams,
their antecedence in the body
one speaks through,
what are its names? soldier
sailor, congressman, spy,
a woman's body is on the table
in the amphitheater of eyes
what to do with it, a ruin,
yet the acoustics are good,
the angel of history
looks in a mirror
remembering the present;

one opens the file
to see how it turns out,
the reviews are not good,
but the enclosures keep sheep
in a formula
the sheep understand,
almost everyone in Philadelphia
reads the *Enquirer*, one is shouting
"fire" in a crowded terminal,
another sleeps on a bench,
the file lists infractions
one refuses to recognize
and perpetuates the replacement
of one with another,
it's in the news.

Redemption

"Devils stroll with angels into our daily lives"
(Fanny Howe)

In the crepuscular hours
they crowd out the blood,
searching for unmarked graves
of unmarked elders,

they hardly had time to forget
their mistakes before being
held to account by their children
or an idea of their children

that keeps him awake
provoking desire for light, heat,
and the paper's
comforting columns,

with death on the right
and suspicion on the left;
I once knew an angel who died
and lives in a city up north,

I once knew a devil who lived
and continues to speak
in the hours before light
of what's lost and what's not.

In Common

So, I signed the form,
relinquished all claims
to future uses of said material
and saved my children

the burden of visiting
these remainders, reminders
of things they have no interest
in protecting

except

I'm trying to reach the 7th floor
but they've moved it
to another part
of the library,

the sign for exit
escapes me
standing in the hall
surrounded by carpet

without a sign,
I think of them
the dreams we have
in common.

THE INAUGURAL

These outsized geographies pass through us
on our way toward some glossy postcard
of a beach offering its exposed and aroused
money

that builds a new machine
to contain its opponents, they think
they're on television turning the wheel
toward paradise when really

continents drift towards each other
until gneiss meets gneiss and
we can be naked again,
watched over

by cameras of solicitude while
vast and invisible suits in tents
invent new countries to fail
and scoop up anyone left behind

for the news, meanwhile
I stumble into exile
with all of its conveniences
listed on the label,

the bombs that have been falling
since we were invented to save
ourselves from each other
have left catacombs of grief our guide

calls history, then, turning to animals
etched on the wall he describes light
the artists imperfectly imagined
and how they blinked

when emerging into night;
if I erase the dates
no one has erected the memorial,
no one is missing

and no one emerges
with a file called the First,
we must be glad
that plenitude has chosen us

as its scribe, the rock
hears everything, the South
is falling into the present
covered in dust, the temples

are stacked in in a warehouse,
waiting for a buyer,
one is on the road
built by the last regime

that is also on the road.

After the Disappearance of Sound

the animal appears who hears
rhymes of blood
surging under skin,
I was

animal in the clearing
where intersecting planes
become myself
or someone wearing my description,

the animal is always there,
a twig breaking
signifies nothing, it leaps
before thought, I thought

nothing satisfies like thinking
of death, nothing accomplishes
matter like an antecedent
searching for its person,

I had this feeling
preceded by I had this flesh, you
were necessary to complete
the conjugation of liquid matter

that coagulates in the public square
where, beneath a castellated wall,
a wolf nursing a city
spills water in a pool.

Voice

"Hearing nothing I am none the less prey to communications"

(Samuel Beckett, *The Unnameable*)

Speechless in Gaza

According to Kierkegaard
the fog came in around 7:00
and lasted all morning,
the crows were squawking.
in the pine across the street,
hawks circling,
neighbors were anxious;

according to the news
the baby
in the bombed hospital
is a lyric subject,
no one hears him
as anything but retribution,
this is what silence sounds like;

dread is the long memory of error
embalmed in alabaster
until night when it returns
with tales of past misdeeds
and crimes; let's destroy a city
and let suffering live, let's repeat
the rhyme and remember Zion;

what's it like to be a thing?
scraps of foreign phrases
in a white bowl
a scarf, the satin Kippot
for special occasions
one of these targets
can be found on Amazon;

the crows caw amassing data
which they freely share,
they don't exist, their goal
is the egg, we who exist
have these words:
why the hawk circles
and the crows cry.

this is what it means
not to be a thing.

Social Media

because something is always out of alignment
causing pain to someone stuck on the 101
on their way late to the dentist offering respite
from unfulfilled expectations at an early age
that continue into this lane where everyone
else drives one of those silver cars,
so you can point out that an infraction
back in the 70s caused irreparable harm
involving a ruptured disk or protestant
letter in that journal still nagging
after all these years and of course
said person is still alive and to all
appearances successful while living
in a town with no post office
no wonder
the water is unsafe to drink at least
we have recourse to shared
community and discussion
untroubled by ego and self-conscious
oblivion.

ABSENT

as the sound of conversation in an adjacent room
is an index of affections shared across a table
among strangers eliciting concern for filling
the space of an hour until the rain stops
with the ambient noise of glasses, footsteps, doors
closing and someone shouting over the din
and the rain coming down on the skylight
preventing night from coming inside
and disturbing this drone
of sociality that serves as a measure
of this matter of attention.

PENSUM

There will be something more
unless this is the last voice
in which case you close the door
and begin again to hear,

someone asks a question
that opens the door
admitting others
who wait outside,

they troop in, the words
you have forgotten to hear
the door, the window, the wall
ands the voice without a sound,

nothing more than thinking
than this will to question,
when will this door open
and who to hear it?

Voices

"... if only this voice could stop, this meaningless voice which
prevents you from being nothing"

Beckett, *The Unnamable*

then something comes into view
like these sentences that disappear and return
upon waking, if only I had committed
those crimes for which I hold myself responsible
each day would hold greater interest
that now is mute on the matter of proof;

there you go, blaming Bob
for his indiscretions while you
have secreted these pages yourself
in a drawer in the secretary
next to the Tiffany lamp that casts
colored light on an intention to stop
distributing stories of flagellation, tales
of blundering youth, it's time to emerge
into silence, turn off the voice
and the voices that demand it.

SELF-IDENTICAL THISNESS

"from voyages between home and not-home..."
(Lyn Hejinian)

You think there's something in-between
to salvage from internecine columns
of print, some hiatus before the image
swims up through the solution
and becomes you on spec,
red cap and blue suit,
Lake Merritt in the background,
the stilled presences, meanwhile March
is full of loss, first L
then T now M, their thisness
pressed between leaves,
a variable life, infrathin,
before speech begins
a pause a rose.

ATELOS

You wait under the blue light of insomnia
for the dream to reveal itself,
a tiny thread
and the warp of yesterday's misery
drops into story;

this is prose talking,
say what you will
it never lives up
to its claims for transparence,

men in red line up for stuff in sacks,
sludge has been floating downstream
since the Directory,
games in the Seine,
insane, they say;

think of misery as a condition of freedom
before it is achieved,
we're waiting for the results
in a period consumed by replacement
you, too, have been replaced,
collect your refund;

stroke upon stroke toward the yellow buoy,
heads in orange caps are waiting,
adequacy is adequate, myopia
a way of seeing through to the other side
they tell you is just ahead.

Dread Seeps In

Children are waiting for a sequel
to the film called "The Anatomy
of Disillusion,"

more bodies disappear
from the cameras installed
on the lamp posts, more migrants

left at the trolley stop;
waiting is the new video
promising shade

not yet available on platforms,
we're waiting for the rain
to stop, sun to fade

under an ancient banyan
scorched by fires,
and the children rapt

in anticipation of the next thing
whatever it is, an algorithm
tells you what you need.

Almost There

These various bodies falling apart
while still thinking, smiling, going
about their business of living,
changing a lightbulb and the form
that requires a new password (where
do all the dead passwords go?),
we sat in the restaurant with a view of the sea
not understanding what was said
but nodding agreeably,
then the bill came as it will,
and one leaves by the side door,
you push but the sign says pull.

TECHNICIAN

In Memory of Jerry Rothenberg

It's so quiet here
you could hear a chickpea drop,
the finches are whooping it up,
setting up shop in the mulberry
where there's enough room for everyone,
down the street
the bins stand at attention
waiting to be dismissed.
April has been arrested,
taking from spring
and its otherwise raucous chant
that voice that sang
"we are birds made of fire"
"Our light is a voice."

Post Script

Poems in *Grace* chronicle a period of gradual hearing loss that began in the mid 1990s and continues into the present day. They attempt to chart the transformations of sounds, inflections, and distortions that make up my daily soundscape. They also chart errors of understanding that begin as what we call "mistakes" or "mishearings" but ultimately become other ways of knowing. A poetics of error recognizes detours in hearing, speaking, and writing as foundational for understanding as one sails (or lurches) towards the horizon of a perfect sentence. There is no such sentence. That horizon is also the illusion of a social totality forged in bonds of solidarity and mutual respect, a social contract being gradually eroded in our current political landscape. What Ilya Kaminsky calls "the Republic of Deafness" is a country under occupation in which its citizens refuse to hear the voice of oppression and adopt deafness as a form of resistance and subversion. The social body begins by recognizing the different body, the one that is never on time, that can't hear the gate change announcement, that speaks out of turn, that flails its arms while walking, that doesn't "fit" in clothing ads. As I say in "My Audiogram," "the body enters the social / in a stave of differences."

The title of section two refers to the drone that defines, for me, the quality of most sounds, a low sustained drone like the *cantus firmus* of early plainsong. But as with early liturgical music, it is a tone upon which other voices are layered, the Psalms sung in varying pitches. These days the drone more often refers to a virtual reality increasingly displacing agency from the actor to the screen, from the battlefield to the technician launching a missile from a bank of computers. One meaning concerns a reduction of pitch and timbre; another is about acting at a distance. Both coincide in a displacement of voice from its source—a distributed voice that speaks in these poems.

A number of poems incorporate signs derived from American Sign Language as mnemonic triggers in my achingly slow learning of that language. In signing "hope" as a fist on a palm or "color" as fingers wiggling at the chin I want to give a kind of secondary materiality to signs whose immediacy, visibility and tactility give body to language. Essential, in this regard, is Christine Sun Kim's observation about the importance of facial expressions as morphological elements in sign language: "Grammar is on your face."

I am grateful to the artist Joseph Grigely for allowing me to include one of his "Conversations" series on my cover. These wall sized installations consist of hundreds of tiny scraps of paper—post its, bar napkins, torn notebook pages—that constitute the partial conversations between deaf and hearing people. Grigely's "Conversations" transform the modernist grid into an echolalic fabric whose fragmentary, incomplete nature bristles with potential—with what is left unsaid.

Poems live at the boundaries of sensation; they register rain before you know it's wet, they register the pulse of a room before the conversation begins. We refer to such moments as impulses or affects, the body's encounter with objects and persons before they have names. Of course, it's hard to keep from filling in the blanks between sensation and meaning—better to live in the interstices, "...internal difference— / Where the Meanings are—," as Emily Dickinson says. Living between deafness and sound, both the audiological and social meanings of these terms, is an interesting condition—a kind of grace—to live a various life.

Solana Beach, CA 12.20.24

MICHAEL DAVIDSON is Distinguished Professor Emeritus at the University of California, San Diego. His work has focused on modern and contemporary American poetry, gender and sexuality studies, disability studies and deaf studies. His books on poetics include *The San Francisco Renaissance: Poetics and Community at Mid-Century* (Cambridge U Press, 1989), *Ghostlier Demarcations: Modern Poetry and the Material Word* (U of California Press, 1997), *Guys Like Us: Citing Masculinity in Cold War Poetics* (U of Chicago, 2003), and *Outskirts of Form: Practicing Cultural Poetics* (Wesleyan U Press, 2011). His work in disability studies includes *Concerto for the Left Hand: Disability and the Defamiliar Body* (U of Michigan, 2008), *Invalid Modernism: Disability and the Missing Body of the Aesthetic* (Oxford U Press, 2019) and *Distressing Language: Disability and the Poetics of Error* (New York U Press, 2022).

He is the author of six books of poetry, the most recent of which is *Bleed Through: New and Selected* Poems (Coffee House Press, 2013). He is the co-author, with Lyn Hejinian, Barrett Watten, and Ron Silliman, of *Leningrad* (Mercury House Press, 1991). He is the editor of *The New Collected Poems of George Oppen* (New Directions, 2002).

www.ingramcontent.com/pod-product-compliance
Lightning Source LLC
Chambersburg PA
CBHW020423130626
46549CB00006B/2707